INSPIRING TRUE STORIES BOOK FOR 7 YEAR OLD BOYS

I AM 7 AND AMAZING

Inspirational tales About Courage, Self-Confidence and Friendship

Paula Collins

© Copyright 2022 - Paula Collins

www.paulacollins.online

paula.collins@paulacollins.online

It is not legal to reproduce, duplicate, or transmit any part of this document in either electronic means or in printed format. Recording of this publication is strictly prohibited and any storage of this document is not al owed unless with written permission from the publisher except for the use of brief quotations in a book review.

This book is a work of fiction. Any resemblance to persons, living or dead, or places, events or locations is purely coincidental.

.

Contents

Introduction   4

Stop Being Invisible   7

Grandma's Birthday   17

Camaraderie and Loyalty: A Tale of
Brotherhood   26

The Thrill of the Giant   38

The Amazing Hidden Talent   45

The Power of Creativity   55

The Music That Heals   65

The Value of True Friendship   75

Swimming in the Air   86

The Cycle of Pets   96

Introduction

Hello, intrepid and wonderful boy! Did you know that you are exceptional? You are unique in the entire universe, which means there is no one like you in this vast world. That's truly amazing! Among billions of people, you have a special way of facing life. You are brave, funny, intelligent, and incredible. Never forget that.

In the world, you will find challenges of all sizes. Some may scare you, while others may make you doubt yourself. But remember, we all feel these emotions. Your parents, siblings, grandparents, friends, and even strangers feel the same as you.

Even when you face your fears, remember that you can overcome them and grow. When trying something new or facing difficult situations, you may feel fear at first, but the experiences that scare you the most often

turn out to be the most valuable. Learn from your mistakes and find the goodness in everything you do, even when things are harder than you imagined.

In this book, you will find stories of children like you, brave and strong, who face situations similar to yours every day. They also feel fear and worry and sometimes don't win, but they work hard, keep trying, and learn from their mistakes until they achieve their goals.

When they feel discouraged or begin to doubt themselves, these children find that unique light within them that helps them keep going, even when they think about giving up. In each story, these children discover self-confidence, hope, and courage that allow them to live incredible experiences in every situation, leading them to reach their dreams.

Now is the time to light up your corner of the world. Share your light with others, free yourself from fear, and learn life's lessons.

Believe in yourself, and you can accomplish anything.

You are an amazing and unique boy!

Stop Being Invisible

Discovering Fear and Invisibility

Hi, I'm James, I'm 7 and a half years old, I live in a loving home with Dad, Mom, and my mischievous cat, Whiskers. I have a superpower that I didn't choose: I can be invisible. Well, not exactly like superheroes, but close. I'm so shy that sometimes I feel like

I disappear, especially when I'm at school or in crowded places.

Today, while looking at the school bulletin board, I saw something that made my heart beat faster: a dance contest. I've always loved dancing. In my room, I become a dance star, where no one can see me. But the idea of dancing in front of others... that's more terrifying than a surprise math test.

The problem is big: on one hand, I want to showcase my dance. On the other, my "invisibility" superpower kicks in when I'm most nervous. How am I going to dance on stage if I can't even raise my hand in class to answer a question?

As I walked home, I thought about all the times I wanted to participate in something and ended up hiding. But this time I feel like it could be different. I want to be seen, I want them to know I exist and that I can do more than just disappear.

My mom says that sometimes we have to face our fears to find out what we're made of. I think it's time to find out what I'm made of. Tomorrow I'm going to sign up for the contest. Well, if my invisibility doesn't decide otherwise.

Can I turn my fear into my dance? I don't know. But one thing's for sure, I want to try. After all, even an invisible superhero has to learn to shine someday.

See you tomorrow. Hopefully with less fear and more courage,

James

The Value of Facing Fear

This morning, after breakfast (my mom made my favorite pancakes to cheer me up), I started practicing my dance. I played my favorite song and imagined myself on stage, under the bright lights. At first, I felt a bit clumsy, like a duck on ice skates. But after a while, I started to feel the music and forgot everything else.

However, every time I remembered that I would have to dance in front of real people, not just my stuffed animals, my heart started

racing like I was in a marathon. "What if I fall? What if everyone laughs at me?" I thought. But then I remembered what Mom said: "Every time you feel afraid, take a deep breath and 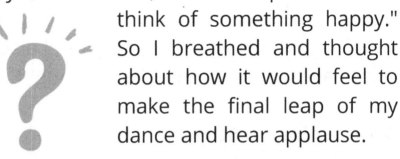 think of something happy." So I breathed and thought about how it would feel to make the final leap of my dance and hear applause.

Mom saw me practicing and said I was doing an incredible job. That made me feel a little better. She taught me some breathing tricks to calm my nerves and told me something I won't forget: "Fear is just a feeling, James. It can't stop you unless you let it."

In the afternoon, while practicing my dance in the garden, something funny happened. I was trying to do a spin and, oops!, I lost my balance and landed on the grass. For a moment, I wanted to disappear out of embarrassment. But then, from the window, I heard Mom laughing and applauding. That made me laugh

too. If I can laugh at my mistakes, maybe the stage won't be so scary after all.

So here I am, ending my day feeling a little braver. Tomorrow I'm going to keep practicing, and who knows, maybe I'll discover that I have more courage than I thought.

Overcoming on Stage

Today was the day of the big dance contest and, wow, what a roller coaster of emotions. The morning started with a knot in my stomach so big I thought I had swallowed a basketball. Seriously, even breakfast seemed like an impossible mountain to climb. "What if I just don't go?" I thought for a moment. But then, I remembered all the times Mom told me that facing my fears is the only way to overcome them.

Getting to the contest venue was like walking towards a giant castle. My legs were shaking so much I almost did a new dance called "the

shakies." Waiting behind the curtain, watching other kids perform their acts, my heart was pounding like a giant drum.

"It's now or never," I told myself. And just before it was my turn, I closed my eyes, took three deep breaths (just like Mom taught me), and thought of my lucky Dinosaur. "Dinosaurs aren't afraid," I told myself.

Then, I heard my name. "James, it's your turn!" I opened my eyes, and with my "brave face" on (the same one I practiced with Mom), I walked onto the stage. The music started, and for a second, all my fear evaporated. It  was just me, the music, and my dance.

I don't know how, but as I danced, I felt like I was flying. Every step, every spin, felt perfect. And when I finished, with a final leap I practiced a thousand times, the room filled

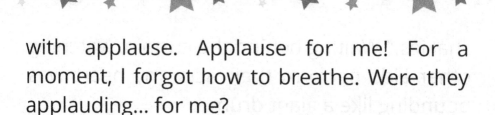

with applause. Applause for me! For a moment, I forgot how to breathe. Were they applauding... for me?

After the performance, several people came to tell me how much they liked my dance. Even Liam, a boy I I met in the hallway, said it was "super cool." I never imagined I could feel this happy and proud of myself.

So here I am, ending the day feeling like a true superstar. I learned that fear is just a ghost that shrinks when you dare to confront it. And that sometimes, all you need to fly is to take the first step... or in my case, the first dance. Now I know that, even though fear may be big, my courage is even bigger.

James's Transformation

After an incredible day, here I am, sitting in my room, thinking about everything that has happened.

Today, as I looked at myself in the mirror, I noticed something different. No, I didn't grow 4 inches overnight (although that would have been awesome), but I did see a James that I didn't know before. A James who dares to dance on stage in front of lots and lots of people.

I thought about all the fears I had before the contest: "What if I mess up? What if everyone laughs? What if...?" But then, I remembered that magical moment on stage, where everything disappeared except the music and me. And I realized something super important: the "what ifs...?"s aren't as terrible as they seem.

I learned that believing in myself is like having a superpower. Yes, it sounds like something a fairytale character would say, but it's true. When you believe you can do something, suddenly the world is filled with possibilities.

Another super important thing I learned is that facing my fears is the only way to overcome them. Yes, it's a bit like facing a giant monster (or a bunch of curious stares), but once you do it, you realize that the monster wasn't as big as you thought.

And here comes the coolest part: being visible has its rewards. After the contest, people who had never talked to me came to say nice things about my dance. I even made some new friends, and that's something the invisible James would never have accomplished!

I'm excited for what's to come. With every new challenge, I know I can grow a little more. And although I know there will be more fears in the future, I also know that I have what it takes to face them.

See you in the next adventure! I'm ready for whatever comes, with a little bit of nerves, of course, but with a lot more courage.

Grandma's Birthday

The Secret Plan of Gabriel

Hello! My name is Gabriel, I'm 7 years old, and I live with my Dad, my Mom, and my little sister Lucy. My favorite place in the whole house is the kitchen because I love helping my mom, who is an expert at cooking delicious dishes. But what I love most of all are her desserts!

Today I'm super excited because I came up with the best idea in the world. Guess what? I'm going to surprise my grandma for her birthday! Not just any surprise, no, no. I'm going to make her chocolate chip cookies because they're her favorite, and because I love it when the kitchen smells like cookies.

My Mom is always making delicious things in the kitchen, and I always watch her do it. Sometimes she lets me help, like when she lets me crack the eggs (although one time I dropped one on the floor, oops!). But this time, I want to do it all by myself to make it a real surprise. Mom says cooking is like doing an experiment that you can eat afterward, and that sounds super fun!

Today at dinner, everyone was talking about grandma's birthday, which is in two days. Dad said we were going to have a big cake and

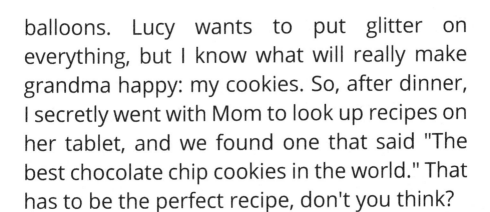

balloons. Lucy wants to put glitter on everything, but I know what will really make grandma happy: my cookies. So, after dinner, I secretly went with Mom to look up recipes on her tablet, and we found one that said "The best chocolate chip cookies in the world." That has to be the perfect recipe, don't you think?

Mom helped me make a list of everything I need: flour, eggs, chocolate chips, and a bunch of other things. Tomorrow, dad will take me to the supermarket to buy everything. It will be like a secret mission!

Well, tomorrow will be a big shopping day, and I can't mess up. Wish me luck on my secret cookie mission!

See you tomorrow!

The Mission of the Burnt Cookies

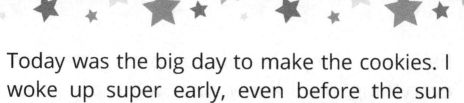

Today was the big day to make the cookies. I woke up super early, even before the sun came up because I was too excited to sleep anymore. Dad and I went to the supermarket and bought everything we needed. I felt like a detective choosing the best ingredients.

When we got back home, I put everything in the kitchen and told mom that today I was going to cook alone. Well, almost alone. She said she would be nearby just in case, especially to use the oven because it's still a little dangerous for me.

I started mixing everything. The eggs, the flour, and the chocolate chips! I followed the recipe step by step, or so I thought. I put the dough on the tray, and mom helped  me put it in the oven. Then, I started talking on the phone with my best friend, Carter. We were talking about a new and super fun game, and... I completely forgot about the cookies!

Suddenly, mom ran to the kitchen because it smelled burnt. The cookies were black! Carter kept talking on the phone, and I could only think about my charcoal cookies. Mom took out the cookies and turned off the oven. It was a disaster.

I felt really sad and almost cried, but then I thought about what my grandpa always says: "If something doesn't go right, try again." So I cleaned everything up and decided to try again. I wouldn't give up!

So here I am ready for the second round. This time without phone calls. Grandma's cookies have to be perfect!

Salt Instead of Sugar

Today was the day of the second attempt at the cookies. I woke up with a lot of desire to do everything right. I put on my

apron, the one that says "Chef Gabriel" (it was a birthday gift), and went straight to the kitchen like a pro.

This time, I checked the recipe twice before starting. I felt like a scientist, making sure every ingredient was perfect. But sometimes even scientists make mistakes...

Well, you know what? I confused salt with sugar! I didn't realize it until the cookies were in the oven and started to smell weird. When we tried them, mom made a very funny face because they were super salty. It was a salty disaster.

I felt really sad and thought about giving up and buying something for grandma's birthday. But then, mom sat down with me and told me something very important: "Gabriel, we all make mistakes, especially when we're learning something new. The important thing is not to give up."

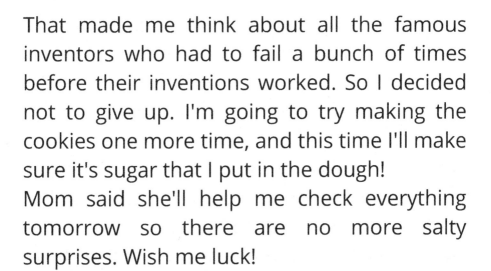

That made me think about all the famous inventors who had to fail a bunch of times before their inventions worked. So I decided not to give up. I'm going to try making the cookies one more time, and this time I'll make sure it's sugar that I put in the dough!

Mom said she'll help me check everything tomorrow so there are no more salty surprises. Wish me luck!

Victory with Cookies!

Today was the day. The day when I finally did it. I woke up even before my alarm clock rang, ready to face my last battle with the cookies. I was determined to make everything perfect this time.

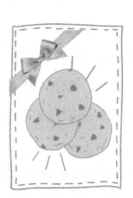

Mom and I checked every ingredient together. "This is sugar," she assured me, and together we put it in the bowl. We followed every step

meticulously, without rushing, remembering the mistakes of the past. I even wore some detective glasses that I found in my drawer to feel more like an ingredient investigator.

When the cookies were in the oven, I stared at the oven door without moving. I wasn't going to allow anything bad to happen to them this time. And when the timer beeped and we took out the cookies, they were perfect! Neither burnt nor salty, just as they should be!

Then came the moment of truth. I packed the cookies in a box that I decorated with drawings of superheroes (because, you know, I felt pretty heroic). I took the box to grandma's birthday party with a big smile.

When we arrived, the whole family was there. I gave grandma her gift. As she opened it, her eyes lit up like Christmas lights. She tried a cookie and then, with a big smile, said, "These cookies are delicious, Gabriel! Did you make them all by yourself?" I told her all about my

adventures in the kitchen and how mom helped me not to give up. We all laughed when I told them about the salty cookies.

Grandma hugged me tightly and said that those cookies were the best gift because they were made with effort and love. And there, I realized something super important: making others happy with something I created made me feel like the happiest kid in the world.

So I learned that even if things don't go well at first, or even the second time, I don't have to give up. Every mistake is just one more step toward doing something great. And the best part is, making someone happy is the best gift I can give (and receive).

Until the next adventure!

Gabriel

Camaraderie and Loyalty: A Tale of Brotherhood

Preparing for Anniversary Week

Hello! My name is John, I'm 7 years old, and I live in a somewhat noisy house with my mom, dad, and my younger brother, who is an expert at mischief-making all day long. We live

in a neighborhood full of kids, but sometimes it feels like I'm the only one interested in following the rules. Dad always tells me, "John, make sure to do the right thing," so I try really hard to be the good boy.

At school, something SUPER important is about to happen: Anniversary Week! It's a whole week without regular classes and full of super fun activities. Everyone is super excited, and so am I!

Most of my classmates... well, let's just say they're not as keen on following the rules as I am. When the teacher leaves the room, it's like a tornado swept through. Everyone starts running and yelling, and they climb on desks as if they were small mountains. I prefer to stay seated, drawing or reading something interesting. Today, for example, I tried to draw a dragon, but it ended up looking like a big duck!

Sometimes I feel a little lonely because I don't join in the mischief. But I also think that being quiet helps me stay out of trouble, and that's good! Besides, drawing duck-dragons isn't so bad.

This year, Anniversary Week seems like it will be more exciting than ever. We're going to have games, food, and even a magician. I can't wait to see what tricks he'll do!

Tomorrow is another day of preparations, and I'm sure my classmates will continue with their craziness. I promise to tell you everything that happens, especially if my duck-dragon improves. Hopefully, I can make friends who also like to draw weird things!

See you tomorrow,

John

Chaos in the Classroom

Today at school, something worthy of an adventure movie (or horror, depending on how you look at it!) happened. The teacher had  to step out for a moment for a meeting with other teachers and left us with only one instruction: "Please, be respectful and stay calm until I return." I think my classmates heard, "Do whatever you want until I come back!"

As soon as she closed the door, it was as if someone had pressed the "madness" button. Timmy launched his eraser into the air like it was a rocket. Then, Lisa and Mark started jumping on their desks as if they were on trampolines. And that wasn't all! A paper battle broke out, and someone (I won't say who, but look where my pen is pointing) even tried to build a fortress with the books.

 Meanwhile, I stayed in my seat, working on my drawing of the duck-dragon, which now has glasses (it gives it an intellectual touch, don't you think?). At one point, some of my classmates came to my desk and asked me to join their "expedition to the other side of the classroom." According to them, it was a journey to discover lost treasures (meaning toys that someone had hidden under the desks).

I confess that for a second, I almost, almost got up and followed them. But then I remembered what my dad always says about following the rules and doing the right thing, even when no one is watching. So, I told them no, with a smile. They left without me, but I think they understood because they gave me a look that said "maybe next time."

I felt a little lonely for not joining in, but also some pride for staying true to my principles. Although being alone sometimes is hard, I know it's important to do what I believe is right. I hope my duck-dragon approves of my decision!

When the teacher returned and saw the mess, her face was priceless. I promise to tell you more tomorrow because it seems like a big storm (of scolding, for sure) is coming.

The Great Disorder and My Great Dilemma

Well, I thought yesterday's chaos was the limit, but today, things got even crazier. The teacher had another one of those meetings (it seems like they have a million of them), and left us alone again. Before leaving, she looked at us very seriously and said, "I expect to find you exactly as I leave you." We all nodded, but I think some crossed their fingers behind their backs.

Not even two minutes after she closed the door, the revolution began. This time, it wasn't just papers flying and people jumping; oh no, some of my classmates decided it would be fun to see what the desks looked like upside down. And they did it! The desks ended up upside down, and the books and notebooks were scattered all over the floor like confetti at a party.

I stayed in my seat, finishing my super drawing of the duck-dragon (now with a superhero cape, just because!). I tried to focus on my strokes and not on the chaos. Although I won't lie to you, a part of me wanted to join in and feel that adrenaline of doing something a little crazy. But, you know? Something inside me said it wasn't right, so I stayed seated.

When the teacher returned and saw the mess, her face turned as red as a tomato. She asked  aloud who was responsible. The whole class fell silent. She even asked me directly, because she knows I'm always attentive. She looked at me with those eyes of "I know you didn't do it, but do you know anything?"

It was so hard not to say anything. I wanted to speak up, tell her everything that happened, but I also knew that would mean ratting out my classmates, and that didn't seem fair to them, even though what they did wasn't right.

I've been thinking a lot about this after school. Dad always says that being loyal is important, but so is being honest. How do you choose? I decided that the best thing I could do was to keep being who I am: someone who tries to do the right thing, even when it's complicated.

Tomorrow is the big day of Anniversary Week, and everyone is super excited. I just hope we can enjoy it without any more problems. And maybe, just maybe, I can find a way to help my classmates understand why it's important to follow the rules.

See you tomorrow!

John

A True Act of Friendship

Today was one of those days that I think I'll never forget. It started with the teacher telling us that unless those responsible for yesterday's disorder confessed, no one would go to Anniversary Week. Everyone stared at the ground, no one wanted to speak. And then, the teacher said that since I always behave well, I would be the only one allowed to attend the event.

I was supposed to feel happy, right? But I didn't. I felt a weird feeling in  my stomach, like I had eaten something I shouldn't have. Seeing my classmates sad and knowing that I would go alone... that didn't seem fair or fun to me.

So I took a deep breath and raised my hand. "Teacher," I said, "I don't want to go to the anniversary if everyone else can't. It wouldn't be the same without my friends." The class fell silent. I could see in my classmates' eyes some surprise and... respect, maybe?

The teacher looked at me, and for a moment, I thought she was going to get angry. But instead, she smiled. "John, that's very noble of you," she said. "If you decide to stay, then everyone will have another chance. But I hope this teaches all of you a lesson about respect and responsibility."

And did the mood change! Everyone started cleaning and tidying up the classroom. Even Timmy, who rarely helps, was organizing the books.

Later, we were all together, laughing, eating treats, and watching the magician pull rabbits out of his hat. It was much more fun because we were all there. And I think today I learned something very important about what it means to be a friend and be part of a team. It's not just about following the rules, but about being there for each other, even when it's hard.

I'm glad I made that decision. At the end of the day, the teacher gave me a pat on the back and said I had done something very mature today. That made me feel even more confident that I had done the right thing.

What a day! Now I'm going to sleep well tonight, with my head full of magic and my

heart full of happiness for having awesome friends.

Until the next adventure!

John

The Thrill of the Giant

The Great Adventure Begins

Hello, I'm Henry, a 7-year-old with an adventurous spirit who absolutely loves amusement parks. I want to share with you the beginning of an incredible story!

The amusement park has finally arrived in town, and I am jumping with excitement. Adventures are my thing, and what's more adventurous than a park filled with rides and attractions? But there's one in particular that has me counting stars before sleep: the Giant Yellow Slide. It's a slide so big it seems to touch the sky. Although I adore facing these kinds of challenges, this one gives me a special tingle in my stomach.

Imagine this: me, Henry, the most adventurous of all, launching myself down that gigantic yellow curve, screaming at the top of my lungs with my arms raised high. It would be the talk of recess for weeks. Of course, as long as I don't close my eyes all the way down. My best friend, Liam, says I'm going to fly like a superhero. I just hope my cape doesn't get tangled.

Although I'm a little nervous (just a little, I promise), I'm determined. Tomorrow, I'm going to face the Giant Yellow Slide and I'm

going to win. Well, at least I'm not going to let it beat me.

So, keep your fingers crossed for me. Tomorrow is the day I become a legend of the amusement park!

A Sea of Adventures and the Giant Yellow Slide

Today dawned a radiant day and it was a day full of adventures in the amusement park. First, I went to the bumper cars, where I felt like a race car driver dodging everyone else. I even won three times in a row! Then, I tried the swinging pirate ship. At first, it was fun to feel how it went up and down, but after the fifth time, my stomach started to think it was in a blender and the breakfast I had in the morning wanted to make its appearance.

Although I had a lot of fun, I couldn't stop looking towards the Giant Yellow Slide. Every time I saw someone slide down it, a part of me wanted to join in and scream with excitement, but another part wanted to run in the opposite direction. It's like having an angel on one shoulder and a little devil on the other, and I can't decide which one to listen to.

Mom says it's okay to be afraid, that it's normal, but also that sometimes, to have fun, we have to face those fears. Although today I didn't become the legend, tomorrow we will go back to the park again and I think it might be the day I finally line up for the Giant Yellow Slide. Wish for the angel to win!

Facing the Giant

I finally gathered all my courage to face the Giant Yellow Slide. While in line,

my legs were shaking like jello on a plate. Every step forward made me want to take two steps back. But then, Mom gave me that little push of bravery I needed.

"Think of this as one of your superhero adventures," mom said. "Even superheroes feel fear, but they overcome it to save the day." That made me smile. Who would have thought that I, Henry, could be a superhero for a day?

When my turn came, I closed my eyes, took three deep breaths as my Mom taught me, and launched myself. For a second, all I could feel was the wind on my face and my heart beating hard. But then, I opened my eyes and... Wow! It was the most exciting ride of my life. In the end, I was so happy I wanted to do it again, so I don't remember how many more times that I went down it!

Thanks to my Mom's advice and my own bravery, today I learned that it's okay to be afraid, but not to let that fear stop you. Thank you, Mom, for helping me see that. The Giant Yellow Slide is nothing compared to the bravery of a boy with an imaginary cape!

Looking Back with Bravery

Today, as I sit here thinking about my adventure with the Giant Yellow Slide, I realize how much I've grown. Facing my fear was not only exciting but also taught me a great lesson about bravery and self-confidence. With my mom's support, I discovered that I can do anything, even if it seems impossible at first.

I've realized that fears are just shadows that become smaller when you decide to face them. And although I know I will encounter many more fears along the way, I now have the bravery to face them one by one.

This journey has taught me that family support is like an invisible superhero cape that always accompanies me. I want to remember this moment every time I face a new challenge.

So, thank you for being here to listen (or rather, read) my adventures. Until the next adventure!

The Amazing Hidden Talent

A Great Challenge on the Horizon

Hello! My name is Jacob, I'm 7 years old, and I live in a small town where almost everyone knows each other. My life is pretty normal: I go to school, play with my friends, and spend time with my family. But there's something I love more than anything else: singing and acting. I feel like a star every time I get to step on a stage or even when I put on small shows in my living room for my parents.

Today at school, our teacher gave us exciting news: we're going to put on a play, and it's not just any play, it's "Romeo and Juliet"! And here's the best part of it all: I was chosen to be Romeo! Imagine, my dream of acting and singing in front of everyone is about to come true.

But not everything is as perfect as it sounds. There's a pretty big "but" in this story, and that "but" has a name: Abby. Yes, you read that right. Abby, the shyest and quietest girl in the whole school, will be my Juliet. The moment the teacher announced her name, I could swear the world stopped for a second. We all stood there with our mouths open, including

her, who seemed to want the earth to swallow her up.

When I got home, I couldn't help but tell my parents everything. My mom, always so positive, told me that maybe this would be a good opportunity for Abby and that I should give her a chance. But, you know? I'm really worried. What if Abby can't overcome her shyness? What if our play doesn't go well because of this? I want it to be perfect, every single day.

I've decided I'm going to do something about it. I can't just sit around waiting for things to fix themselves. Tomorrow, I'm going to talk to Abby before rehearsals. Maybe, between the two of us, we can find a way to make her feel more comfortable on stage.

Action plan: Turn Abby into the best Juliet our little town has ever seen. It's time to act, in every sense of the word!

With determination,
Jacob, the Romeo with a mission.

A Musical Surprise

Today was one of those days that made you see everything differently. After class, I went to Abby's house to practice our parts of the play. I was super nervous. Not just about the rehearsal, but about how we were going to work together.

Abby lives in a house that looks like it's from a storybook, with a garden full of flowers and a stone path leading to the door. Her mom greeted me with a huge smile and led me to her room. And here's the incredible part!

When I opened the door, Abby was playing the piano! But not just anything... she was playing one of the songs from our play, and it sounded...

magical. I never would have imagined that the shy girl in class had a talent like that. It was like discovering that my classmate was a musical superhero.

I couldn't help it; I stood there, wide-eyed, listening to her play until she finished. And when she did, I applauded her as if I were at the most impressive concert of my life. Abby blushed a lot and told me she felt embarrassed to play in front of others. Embarrassed! With that talent, she should be giving concerts.

So, right then and there, my mission changed. It was no longer just about making our play a success. Now it was also about helping Abby share her incredible talent with everyone. The world needs to hear her!

We practiced together, and believe me, when Abby forgets about her fear, it's like she transforms. In fact, she even taught me some tricks with her voice. Turns out, she's not only

a piano genius, she also knows a lot about singing. Who would have thought!

At the end of the day, I went home with a mix of excitement and admiration. Abby is not only going to surprise everyone in the play, I think we're going to make a spectacular team. And to think that all this time she was there, hidden behind her shyness.

So never underestimate anyone. Everyone has something special to show.

With enthusiasm,
Jacob, the talent detective turned singer.

The Day of the Big Surprise

Today was the big day of the play, and I have so much to tell you. I was so excited and nervous that I could hardly eat breakfast. But the most important thing today wasn't my nervousness, but what happened with Abby.

We arrived early at school, and the gym was already transformed into a big theater. Behind the stage, we were all a little nervous, but no one was more than Abby. I saw her there, as quiet as always, and I thought, "Today, everyone is going to see how amazing she is."

And then, the play began. Everything was going well, and the most awaited moment arrived: the first song. I took a breath, looked at Abby, and something magical happened. When the music started, Abby transformed. She wasn't the shy girl we all knew. She was... a rockstar Juliet! She sang with such a loud and clear voice that for a second, everyone was silent, as if they couldn't believe what they were hearing.

And then, applause! Lots and lots of applause. Our classmates, the teachers, the parents, everyone was on their feet, applauding like crazy. It was the most amazing moment of my life.

After the play, everyone wanted to talk to Abby, congratulate her, and ask her how long she has known how to sing like that. I saw the surprise on their faces, just like the surprise I had the first day I heard her. And Abby, well, she just smiled, a little overwhelmed, but happy.

Now, I'm more excited than ever for what's to come. Because after today, I know there are stories, talents, and surprises waiting for us, we just have to be ready to discover them.

With a heart full of music and surprises,
Jacob, the talent detective and Abby's number one fan.

A Bunch of New Things

Today, I'm thinking about everything that has happened these last few days. It was a huge adventure, full of music, nerves, and a big

surprise named Abby. After yesterday's play, I've been reflecting a lot on everything I learned.

We should never, ever judge people just by how they look or what we think we know about them. Abby taught me that. And today's play... well, it showed everyone that everyone has something special and something shining, inside. We just need the opportunity to let it out.

Then there's the issue of fear. I was afraid of how the play would turn out, and Abby was afraid of showing herself as she is. But together, we learned that facing those fears makes us stronger. It's like when you swing to the highest point and feel like you're going to fly; it's a little scary, but also super exciting.

I also learned about empathy and courage. Helping Abby feel safe and seeing how everyone changed their opinion about her was

something very special. It reminded me that everyone carries something cool inside, it's just that sometimes we need a little help to show it. It's like when you team up at recess and realize that together, everyone has more fun.

So, here I go, ready for whatever comes, with my ears open to listen to more stories and my heart ready to meet more friends like Abby. Because now I know that every day can be an adventure, and I'm excited to discover what surprises await me.

With a little song in my heart and a bunch of new ideas in my head,

Jacob

The Power of Creativity

Quest for Adventure on a Boring Day

Hello, I'm Daniel, I'm 7 years old, and I live in a cozy house with my parents and my dog Max, who is quite mischievous. From my room, which is filled with toys and adventure books, I can see our garden, which often becomes my exploration field.

Today is one of those days that seems like it will last forever. I'm sitting at the old plastic table in the backyard. Yes, the same one we use for barbecues and that seems to have survived more battles than a superhero. My friend Lisa is here with me.

I've started tapping my fingers on the table. Tap-tap-tap. Lisa says the sound is annoying, but I only do it because there's nothing better to do. I'm so bored I could watch a snail race and find it exciting!

Lisa finally sighs. "I can't stand this boredom anymore," she says. I tell her, "That makes two of us." We look around. Everything in the backyard seems so normal and boring... the same old table, the same old chairs, the same old patio.

Then Lisa has an idea. "What if we go out and look for something to do?" It's not the worst idea, so we leave the backyard through the little gate that leads to the alley and start walking around the neighborhood.

First, we went to Mary's house, but she was busy helping her mom with cookies. Then we tried Victor's house, but no one was home. The same at Louisa's house: her mom said she had too much homework. It seems like everyone has something to do, except us.

After walking for a while, we arrived at Lisa's uncle's house. He was outside, moving a huge wardrobe. "What are bored kids like you doing around here?" he asked us with a smile. We told him we were super bored and didn't know what to do.

Lisa's uncle scratched his head and then said something that made me think. "When I was a kid, I was never bored. I always found something fun to do." He suggested we play soccer, but he was too busy to join.

So Lisa and I looked at each other and then, without saying much, started using our

imagination. Who needs toys when you have a whole park to turn into a magical kingdom or a jungle full of wild animals?

Let's see where this adventure takes us. Maybe this day won't be so boring after all.

Adventures in the Magical Forest of the Park

Lisa and I arrived at the park and decided it was time to leave boredom behind once and for all. After walking around aimlessly for a while, I had a brilliant idea: why not turn the local park into our own magical world? And that's exactly what we did!

 We imagined the park was an enchanted forest full of mysterious creatures and challenges to overcome. Lisa put a leaf on her head and said it was her forest queen crown. I found a stick that looked like an

ancient sword, so I decided I would be a brave knight.

Our first "trial" was to cross the "Great Wild River," which was actually the stream that runs through the park. We managed to cross by jumping from stone to stone. Well, Lisa almost fell into the water, but I caught her just in time. She said that's what real knights do.

Just as we were celebrating our victory over the Great River, a "stern forest steward" appeared. He was just an old man walking his dog, but in our adventure, he became the guardian of the castle gates. He politely asked us to pick up some branches blocking the path. Of course, we completed the task with honor.

Then, as we explored the "Enchanted Thicket," we came across a bright fairy. It was actually just a pretty big butterfly fluttering around the flowers, but in our imagination, it was leading us to a hidden treasure.

We had so much fun that we didn't even notice hours had passed. It was amazing how the park transformed into a place full of magic and adventure. Sometimes, all you need is a little imagination to turn a normal day into something extraordinary.

Tomorrow, we'll continue our exploration. Who knows what other wonders we'll discover in our enchanted forest!

Meeting the Forest Guardian and the Treasure Keeper

Today is our second day of imagination, and it was filled with more adventures in our enchanted forest! Lisa and I returned to the park, and just when we started to think we had seen everything there was to see, we met someone very special.

We met a "magical woman" who, in reality, was Mrs. Emma, who always brings her ice cream cart to the park. But in our adventure, she became the Forest Guardian, a wise lady who

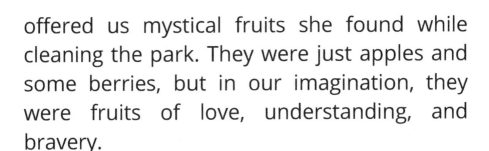

offered us mystical fruits she found while cleaning the park. They were just apples and some berries, but in our imagination, they were fruits of love, understanding, and bravery.

Each "magical fruit" gave us special powers. The apple was the Fruit of Love, which made us love our friends and family even more. The berries were the Fruit of Understanding, which helped us understand the mysteries of the forest. And a banana was the Fruit of Bravery, to face the greatest challenges!

And speaking of challenges, the biggest one came afterward. At the end of the forest (well, the park), we found the Treasure Keeper, a "giant" who was actually my dad, who had come to look for us because it was time to go home. In our story, he guarded the Fruit of Wisdom, which was a huge orange he had brought for our snack.

To be able to take the Fruit of Wisdom, we had to answer a riddle he asked us. The riddle was: 'What has leaves but is not a tree?' It took us a while, but in the end, Lisa guessed it was a book. Dad laughed and gave us the orange!

It was amazing how our simple walk turned  into an adventure full of magic and challenges. We learned that with a little imagination, we can transform any place into a world of adventure. And also that the most important fruits are the ones we share with others, like love, understanding, and bravery.

Tomorrow will be another day, and who knows what adventures await us on our next trip to the enchanted forest!

Reflections of a Knight and a Forest Queen

After two days filled with adventures in our "enchanted forest," Lisa and I sat down today at the same old plastic table to talk about

everything we had done. I can't believe that at the beginning of this week, all we could say was "I'm bored."

Reflecting on our days of play, we realized how powerful imagination can be. We turned an ordinary park into a kingdom full of magic, challenges, and mysterious characters. And although it was just our local park and some adults playing along with our ideas, for us, it was like visiting another world.

We learned that you don't need expensive things or to go to faraway places to have great adventures. Sometimes, all you need is a friend and the willingness to see things differently. Imagination took us to places we could never visit otherwise.

Today, as we ate the last piece of the Fruit of Wisdom (the orange dad gave us), Lisa and I made plans for our next adventure. Maybe

next time we can turn the basement into a dragon's cave or the attic into a castle tower.

I want to always remember how something as simple as a boring day turned into one of the best weeks of my life, all thanks to a little creativity and a lot of laughter. I hope we never forget how to use our imagination to make every day special.

So, even though today we close the book on our adventure in the enchanted forest, I know it's only the beginning of many more stories we'll write together. Imagination is the key, and the world is our castle!

Until the next adventure,

Daniel

The Music That Heals

The Big Fear of Owen

Hello! My name is Owen and I'm 7 years old. I want to share something with you that really bothers me: hospitals! Yes, I know it sounds weird because nothing bad has ever happened to me in one, but just the idea of going makes me feel like I have giant butterflies in my stomach. And not the good kind.

Well, things get worse. My favorite uncle, Uncle John, is in the hospital because he's having surgery for appendicitis. That means I have to visit him. Yes, just me, Owen, the guy who is super scared of hospitals.

My mom says I need to be brave and that Uncle John will be really happy to see me. But all I can think about are those huge automatic doors, the smell of medicine, and worst of all, the needles! Although Mom insists that nothing will happen to me because we're just visiting.

Today at dinner, I tried to convince my parents to let me stay home and play video games instead of going to the hospital, but it didn't work. So it looks like there's no escape. Tomorrow is the big day and I'm already nervous.

I'm going to bring my portable game console and my headphones. Who knows, maybe I can

hide in a corner and play until it's time to leave. Or maybe, just maybe, I might find something there that's not as bad as I think.

Well, wish me luck. I'm going to need it.

Hospital Exploration Mission

Today was THE day. Yes, the day I had to go to the hospital to see Uncle John. I woke up with a knot in my stomach and spent about an hour deciding what to bring. In the end, I grabbed my portable game console, my headphones, and a couple of comics, just in case I needed an emergency distraction.

Mom insisted that I had nothing to fear, that we were just visiting and that no one was going to come at me with a needle. But still, I couldn't stop thinking about all those hospital stories I'd heard.

We arrived at the hospital and everything was as I remembered: long hallways, strange smells, and that feeling that everyone knows something you don't. We went straight to my uncle's room, and although I was happy to see him, I couldn't stop looking around for hidden syringes.

Uncle John and Mom started talking about adult stuff, like the operation and hospital things. I tried to listen, but their words started to sound like when adults in movies talk a lot and you don't understand anything after five minutes. So I decided it was time for a little adventure.

I escaped under the guise of going to the bathroom and began exploring the hallways. The great thing about hospitals is that there's always something going on. I passed a room where a boy was watching a superhero show I liked, so I stayed for a while watching from the door until a nurse saw me and smiled. I guess I didn't look as suspicious as I felt.

As I walked, I started to realize that not everything in the hospital is so bad. There were a lot of people smiling, some nurses were playing with a little boy in the hallway, and I even saw a doctor giving a balloon to another kid.

Then, just as I was about to head back, I heard music. Yes, music in the hospital. It wasn't coming from a radio but from someone playing live. I followed the sound until I found the source: a girl in one of the rooms was playing the guitar. I peeked in a little and... well, it turns out it wasn't just any music, it was a girl named Luna playing guitar in her room.

A Musical Duo in the Hospital

Luna was there because she had to stay in the hospital for a long treatment, but she didn't seem sad at all. Actually, she was filling the place with music and joy. She told me that music helped her feel better and forget about being sick.

Luna had her guitar next to her and asked if I knew how to play any instruments. I told her I knew a bit of piano, and then she smiled and asked me to sing with her. I was nervous, but how could I say no?

So there we were, in the middle of a hospital, giving a mini-concert. Luna played the guitar and I sang. I didn't know I knew so many songs until I started singing. We went from one song to another, and some patients peeked out their doors to listen.

Suddenly, we had a small audience: patients, doctors, and visitors. Everyone listened and some even applauded. I never thought I'd say this, but for a moment, the hospital didn't seem like such a bad place.

Luna taught me that even in tough situations, you can find something that makes you happy and share it with others. Playing and singing with her made me forget my fear, and for a while, all I cared about was the music.

When I finally went back to my mom and Uncle John, I told them all about Luna and how we had made music together. My uncle said he was proud of me for being so brave and trying something new.

Today I learned that hospitals are not just places where you get healed, but also where you can make friends and find new ways to be brave. And maybe, just maybe, they aren't so scary after all.

Tomorrow I'll go back to visit my uncle and I hope to see Luna again. I can't wait to tell you more about my adventures.

Until tomorrow,

Owen

Songs that Change Everything

Today they told my uncle he could go home soon. He's much better, and I think part of that is thanks to the mini-concert we gave him. He said that Luna's music and my singing helped him feel better faster. That made me feel amazing.

So today is the last day of my hospital visit, and I must say I never thought I'd be a little sad to not come back. If you had told me a week ago that I would find something good in the hospital, I would have thought you were crazy. But here we are.

After spending these days with Luna and seeing how her music changed the atmosphere of the hospital, I've started to think differently about many things. Not just about hospitals, but also about how I face things that scare me.

Luna and I spent the morning playing music again. Some patients who already recognized us even requested songs, and I felt like we

were some kind of musical superheroes. There was nothing better than seeing someone who wasn't feeling well smile. It  made me forget I had ever been afraid of being there.

I've learned that often, fear is just in our heads. And that with friends and something you're passionate about, you can face almost anything. Today, instead of hiding from doctors or nurses, I greeted them. I even thanked them for taking care of everyone here, including my uncle John.

So I'm thinking about how I can keep doing what Luna does. She says she'll continue playing her guitar even after she leaves the hospital. And I've decided that I want to keep singing, not just at home, but maybe also in other places where I can help make people smile.

Luna and I have made plans to keep in touch and maybe come back to the hospital from time to time to play music together. She says we're a team now, and I think she's right. Together we can do much more than we could do alone.

Thank you for being here to listen to all this. It's been a crazy week, but I've learned a lot. More than anything, I've learned that with a little music and friendship, you can change the world, or at least change the way you see it.

Until next time,

Owen

The Value of True Friendship

Ethan and the New Classmate

My name is Ethan, I'm 7 years old, and I live in a small town with my mom and dad, who are always trying to teach me things about life... although I already know quite a bit, especially about how to keep things perfect. Today was one of those days that make you want to stay in bed... but for some reason, I always end up getting up.

If there's something that really matters to me, it's keeping everything clean and orderly. I like my hair to be perfect (thank you, gel) and my clothes without a single wrinkle. Mom says I'm a bit obsessive, but what does she know about school fashion?

Well, everything was going as usual at school, mastering the art of being tidy and avoiding the chaos that is recess, when suddenly... bam! A new kid in class. And not just any kid. I'm talking about the kind of kid who looks like he's been in a fight with a tornado... and lost.

Everyone was whispering about him, wondering who he was and why he was so quiet. His name is Alex, and to be honest, when I saw him, I almost fell out of my chair (and that would have ruined my perfect morning pose!). His hair was like a bird's nest, and his shirt looked like it had been white... in another life.

 And the smell? It was like sweaty socks after a soccer game and some old sneakers had decided to throw a party. Yes, that intense. When he sat next to me, I almost passed out. I thought about all the ways to escape, but then I remembered what mom always says: "Be polite, Ethan." So, I took a big gulp of air (from my shirt, not from the air) and decided to face the day.

"Hello!" he said with a giant smile. "I'm Alex."

"Uh, hi," I managed to say, keeping my distance.

"How about we be friends?" he proposed.

I just raised my eyebrows. Being friends with the tornado kid wasn't on my to-do list. But there I was, trying not to breathe too much, and thinking about how I would survive the rest of the day.

So, today I learned that school can be a place full of surprises... and not all of them pleasant.

Tomorrow I'll bring my own disinfectant, just in case. And who knows, maybe this Alex has something interesting to offer, besides his "unique" aroma.

See you tomorrow!

Ethan's Nose Battle

 Today I went back to school armed with my favorite perfume bottle (the one that smells like "space adventure," whatever that means) and a determined mindset to survive another day next to Alex.

The truth is, today was even tougher. Not only did I have to face the challenge of being close to Alex and his smell of "old sneaker party," but also, seeing him up close, I noticed more things that made me want to run to the nurse's office and ask for an oxygen mask. His nails were so dirty they looked like little maps of muddy roads, and his shirt, well, I think it has seen better days.

I tried to focus on my work, but it was hard with Alex so close. Every now and then, he tried to start a conversation, throwing comments like "Did you see the game last night?" or "I really like this class, how about you?" I couldn't help but wonder how someone who doesn't seem to care about his appearance could be so... friendly.

My mom always says I should be polite and courteous, but this is testing all the courtesy lessons mom has taught me so far. Every moment of the day, I had to remind myself not to judge Alex just by how he looks or smells... although it's VERY difficult.

The worst part came when we had to do a project in pairs. Guess who was my partner. That's right! So there I was, trying not to breathe too much while we worked together. But something weird happened. The more we talked, the less bothered I was by the smell. It's not like it disappeared, but I guess I was getting used to it. Or maybe, just maybe, I was starting to see Alex as more than just bad smells and old clothes.

At the end of the day, when mom came to pick me up, she found me smiling. I found out that Alex is really funny and knows a lot about dinosaurs, which happens to be one of my favorite topics.

"Mom," I said in the car on the way home, "I think Alex might be my friend, after all."

She just smiled and said, "I told you people are more than their appearance, Ethan."

So, although I'm still learning to deal with the "Alex aroma," I'm also learning that making a new friend can be worth it... even if you have to hold your breath a little from time to time.

See you tomorrow!

Mom's Lesson

Today was another one of those days that make you wonder if you're really ready to be an adult. Because being an adult seems like a lot of work, especially when it comes to understanding people.

After school, I came home dragging my feet and feeling like I was carrying a sack of potatoes on my back. The day with Alex was, well... a challenge. Not because he did anything wrong, but because I couldn't stop thinking about what mom had told me the day before.

I got home and mom was in the kitchen. She must have some kind of radar because as soon as I crossed the door, she asked me how my day had gone. I told her about Alex and how I had tried to be friendly, but that the smell and his appearance made it really difficult.

Mom stopped what she was doing and looked at me with that look that means an important lesson is coming. "Ethan," she said, "sometimes people go through things that we

can't see just by looking at them. Have you ever wondered why Alex might look like that?"

I shook my head. Honestly, I hadn't thought about it. I was too busy trying not to breathe through my nose.

"Ethan, not everyone has the same things you do. Not everyone has someone to wash their clothes or buy them new shoes when they need them," mom continued. "Maybe Alex is going through something difficult. Maybe he needs a friend more than ever."

That idea made me feel a little ashamed. I hadn't thought of Alex as someone who might need help. I just saw him as a problem I had to endure.

So, after talking to mom, I decided that tomorrow I'm going to do something different. Not only am I going to try to be friends with Alex, but I'm also going to try to understand

him a little better. Who knows, maybe I can help him in some way.

Mom smiled at me and gave me one of those hugs that seem to fix things a little. "I'm proud of you," she said. And for the first time in a long time, I felt really good about school, despite everything else.

Well, tomorrow will be a new day, and I'll face it with a little more understanding and a little less complaining about the smell. After all, as mom says, we're all dealing with something.

See you tomorrow!

A New Friend on the Horizon

If you had told me a week ago that Alex would become one of my friends, I probably would have laughed. But look, here we are, and I have to tell you, it's been quite a journey.

Today, Alex and I spent more time together. Not only in class, but also at recess. I learned a lot about him. For example, his mom works a lot and Alex has to do a lot of things on his own

at home, like making his food and taking care of his clothes. That explains a lot about why things are the way they are for him.

When I told him how I felt at first about his appearance and smell, Alex just laughed. "That's just part of my daily adventure," he said. I don't know why, but that made me see everything differently. It's not that I suddenly like the smell of dirty laundry, but I understood that there's more to Alex than just that.

Plus, I found out that Alex is incredibly funny and knows a lot about things I didn't even know interested me, like the history of video games and how to fix bikes. He's also pretty good at making up stories; together we came up with one about a superhero who fights villains with the power of laughter. Who knew he had so much imagination?

Reflecting on this week, I realize how easy it is to judge someone just by how they look on the outside. My mom was right, people are more than their appearance, and sometimes,

circumstances can make life a little more complicated for some.

I'm grateful for giving Alex a chance and for learning a big lesson about friendship and empathy. Not only have I gained a new friend, but I've also learned to look beyond what meets the eye.

Thank you for being here to listen to all of this. I can't wait to see what other adventures await me with Alex. Who knows, maybe one day we'll write a book about our crazy stories.

Until next time,

Ethan.

Swimming in the Air

The Great Problem of the Ghost Pool

Hello! My name is Mark, I'm 7 years old, and I live in a small town with my parents and my younger sister, Lucy. Everyone knows each other here because, well, there aren't many of us! And although I love where I live, there's always been something that bothers me: we only have one public pool and it's almost always crowded.

Today was a SUPER weird day. After a lot of insisting, my parents finally agreed to enroll me in the town's swimming school. Imagine my excitement! I arrived with my swimsuit, my goggles, and even my new glow-in-the-dark fins, thinking I was going to become a fish in the water.

But here's the weird part. Turns out we weren't going to swim in water. The coach, a man who looks older than my grandpa and is always frowning, told us that first we have to learn to "swim on dry land." He took us to a gym that smelled like feet and made us lie down on wooden benches to move our arms and legs as if we were in the water. Not a single drop of water in sight!

My friends and I looked at each other like saying "is this guy okay?" I wanted to dive into

the water, feel like a fish, but instead, there I was, making a fool of myself, moving my arms in the air.

I asked the coach when we were going to swim for real, and he just said "all in due time" and that "dry land swimming would make us champions." Maybe he doesn't know how to turn on the pool heater, or something like that.

So here I am, trying to learn to swim, but without touching the water. I hope tomorrow at least they let us dip our feet. Or that someone reminds the coach that swimming is supposed to be in the water!

See you tomorrow!

Mark

Adventures in Swimming... But Without Water

Today was my second day at swimming school, and I have to say it was even weirder

than the first. I arrived loaded with my swimming gear ready to dive into the pool, and guess what? We still didn't need to use it! Yes, another day on solid ground, and I'm starting to wonder if someone forgot to tell me that this is a swimming school without water.

The coach, who is more serious than a pop quiz at school, made us do warm-ups that seemed more suitable for astronauts than swimmers. We ran around the gym, did jumping jacks, and then we were made to "swim" on wooden benches. We had to imagine we were in the water, moving our arms and kicking. All very strange.

I'm starting to think that this coach might be an inventor trying to figure out how to make people swim through the air. If that's the case, I think he should tell us, because all my friends are confused too.

While "swimming" on the benches, the coach walked around, adjusting our movements and

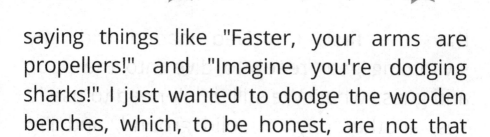

saying things like "Faster, your arms are propellers!" and "Imagine you're dodging sharks!" I just wanted to dodge the wooden benches, which, to be honest, are not that comfortable.

At the end of class, I was so frustrated that I told the coach that I didn't understand how this would help us become better swimmers. He just frowned and said that "patience is a virtue in water and on dry land." Well, I think I'm going to need a lot of patience with this swimming school.

Tomorrow, I hope I finally see some water, even if it's in a glass. Keep your fingers crossed for me!

See you later,

Mark

Dry Land Swimming Reaches New Heights

Today at "swimming" school (if we can even call it that), things got even more intense. The coach must think we're training to be superheroes or something, because every day the exercises become more complicated and I just want to jump into a real pool.

We started the class with our usual warm-up that already seems like a magical ritual to summon water, but, spoiler: no water appeared. Then, the coach got serious with the technical movements. Today was all about coordinating breathing with arm movements, which, I have to admit, is pretty tough when you're lying on a wooden bench.

I tried to do everything the coach said: breathe when you raise your right arm, exhale when you lower it, don't forget to smile while you suffer... Well, he didn't say that last part, but he probably thought it. And believe me, it's much harder than it sounds, especially when you're trying not to fall off the bench.

I came home feeling like I had run a marathon on another planet. Everything hurt, and I

wasn't sure I could move tomorrow. I told my dad how I felt and about my doubts with these dry land workouts. He listened to me, gave me one of those "I understand, son" looks, and said something that really made me think. "Mark, sometimes coaches have different methods, but there's a reason behind it all. Give it a chance and keep trying. You might surprise yourself with what you can achieve."

So, despite my doubts and wanting to give up my dream of being a swimmer because of the wooden benches, I decided to push through. Somehow, my dad's words gave me a glimmer of hope. And you have to admit, it would be pretty cool to say that I learned to swim in the air before mastering the water.

Tomorrow is another day, and who knows, maybe I'll finally see a drop of water. Or maybe learn to fly, considering how things are going!

See you tomorrow,

A Leap of Faith on Dry Land

Today we wrapped up our last day of dry land training, and although it may seem incredible, I'm starting to think that all this business of swimming in the air wasn't so crazy after all. Yes, I know it sounds strange coming from me, who has spent the last entries complaining about not touching water.

Reflecting on these past few days, I realize how much I've learned. Not only about how to move my arms and breathe as if I were underwater, but also about how to face things that don't make much sense at first. My coach, that serious man who seems like an ancient book of swimming secrets, always used to say, "Trust the process, Mark." And well, I think he was right.

I've discovered that sometimes the most important lessons aren't the most obvious ones. At first, I couldn't understand how waving my arms and legs in the air would help

me in a pool. But now I see that all that dry land exercise has made me stronger and taught me to control every movement and breath. It's like learning to walk before you run, just with more imaginary floaties.

My dad always says that adaptability is one of those super important skills you need in life. And now, after all this, I'm starting to believe it. Adapting to swimming on dry land has shown me that I can handle new and difficult things, and that makes me feel ready for anything, even the swimming tests coming up soon.

So, although I miss the water and can't wait to dive into a real pool, I'm grateful for these lessons. They've been weird, tough, and sometimes painful, but also incredibly useful.

I'm excited for the tests and to show what I've learned. Maybe, just maybe, this strange training will be the thing that helps me shine. And who knows, if all goes

well, maybe one day, this dry land training will be my secret to winning medals.

Thank you for listening. See you in the pool... at last!

Until the next adventure,

Mark

The Cycle of Pets

The Mission of Having a Pet

Hello, my name is Lucas, I'm 7 years old, almost 8, and I have a mission in life: to have my own pet. Not just any pet, but the best pet in the world. Although, to be honest, any little animal would make me the happiest boy on the planet.

My love for animals is huge. As big as the elephant I saw the other day at the zoo, who, by the way, looked at me as if he understood my dream. Sometimes, I imagine that wild animals are like my stuffed animals. For example, I think that lions have manes as soft as my favorite teddy bear, and that if I hug a real bear, it would be like hugging a big warm cushion.

But here comes the problem. My parents aren't very convinced about the idea of having animals at home. They say that dogs are naughty and that cats sharpen their claws on all the furniture. Even fish are out of the question because, according to them, cleaning an aquarium is harder than solving a math puzzle. And they won't even let me start talking about having a snake. Imagine that!

Today, while walking home from school, I saw a little dog on the street wagging its tail like a fan. It was love at first sight. I said to him, "Someday, I'll have my own little dog, and I promise it won't be as naughty as my parents

say." The little dog just licked my hand as if to say, "I believe you, Lucas!"

So, I've decided that I'm going to prove to my parents that I can be responsible. I've come up with a master plan: I'll take care of the plant in the living room for a week without forgetting to water it a single day. If I succeed, I'll show them that I'm ready to have a pet.

Puppy Rescue Operation

Today has been the most incredible and terrifying day of my life! And all thanks to a little furry encounter. But let me tell you from the beginning.

I was walking home after school, thinking about my big plant plan (which, by the way, is still alive and kicking... well, plants don't have tails, but you get the idea). Suddenly, I heard a strange sound. It wasn't like the usual sounds I hear on my daily adventure home, like Mr. Jenkins

scolding his cat or Mrs. Miller practicing opera (which sounds more like a cat scolding Mr. Jenkins).

No, this sound was a cry. A soft and sad cry that caught my attention. I followed the sound until I found a wet box behind a garbage container. And there, looking at me with the saddest and most beautiful eyes I've ever seen, was a puppy. A puppy! Alone and scared, but so, so adorable.

My heart said, "Lucas, this is the moment! It's your destiny!" But my brain said, "Wait a minute! Don't you remember the 'no pets' rule at home?" Well, at that moment, my heart won by a landslide.

I knew my parents wouldn't be happy, but something inside me couldn't leave that poor puppy there. So, I did what any hero in an epic story would do: I wrapped him in my jacket, put him in my backpack (with his head sticking out so he could breathe, of course), and took him home. I named him Toby, because every hero needs a cool name.

Getting home was the hardest part. Every time Toby moved, I made noises like coughing or singing to cover up any sound he made. I think my mom now thinks I'm a beginner in some kind of music.

Once in my room, I created the perfect shelter for Toby in my closet. I gave him some milk (because that's what they do in movies, right?) and found an old toy for him to play with. Toby seemed happy, and I felt like the best person in the world.

But here comes the terrifying part: I have to keep Toby a secret. My plant care plan has just turned into a secret puppy care mission. And I have to do it right, because Toby depends on me. And not only that, I have to keep the plant alive too. Being responsible is exhausting.

I promise to keep you informed of how everything goes.

Secret Puppy Mission

Today has been like living in a spy movie, but instead of spying, my mission is to keep an adorable and secret puppy happy and safe! Taking care of Toby is turning out to be an adventure with more twists and turns than my favorite slide in the park.

First, the food challenge. Did you know that puppies eat as if they've never seen food before? Well, Toby is exactly like that. I've had to be super careful to get him something to eat without my parents noticing. This morning, while they were preparing breakfast, I made my boldest move: "accidentally" dropped some of my toast on the floor. Then, I quickly picked it up and hid it for Toby. Mission accomplished!

But, here comes the tricky part. Toby is a very playful puppy, and, well, he doesn't quite understand the whole silent secret agent thing. Today, while I was doing my homework,

he started barking because he wanted to play. I almost had a heart attack! I had to make up that I was practicing sound effects for a school play. I'm not sure if my mom completely bought it, but luckily, she didn't ask any more questions.

Heat is another big issue. Toby likes to snuggle in warm places, and my room can be a little cold. So, I've created a little nest with blankets and my warm pajamas. I know it's not ideal, but so far, it seems to work. Toby curls up there and falls asleep right away, which gives me a little breathing room.

Despite the challenges, I fall more in love with Toby every day. Every time he looks at me with those big shiny eyes, I feel like all this effort is worth it. I want to show that I can be responsible, not only for Toby but also to show my parents that I can take care of a real pet.

For now, I have to keep being the best secret puppy caregiver in the world. And that means always being one step ahead, like a true pet ninja. Who would have thought that having a

puppy would be so exciting and exhausting at the same time?

A Scare and a Hope

Today has been the hardest day of my life. I never thought I would have to write about something like this, but here I am, trying to find the right words. This morning, when I went to greet Toby, I found him very still. He wasn't moving, and no matter how much I called him, he didn't react. My heart shattered into a thousand pieces. Toby had gotten sick.

I ran to tell my mom, with tears in my eyes and my heart shattered. I was preparing for a scolding for keeping Toby a secret, but instead, she hugged me tightly. After listening, she said, "Let's take him to the vet, quickly. We have to do everything we can to help him." I felt immense relief and a glimmer of hope.

At the vet, while we waited, mom held my hand and said, "Lucas, taking care of someone means doing the right thing, even when it's difficult. You've shown a lot of love and bravery by bringing Toby." I learned that asking for help is as important as giving it.

The vet gave us good news after examining Toby. With medicine and care, he could recover. I will never forget that feeling of gratitude and relief.

The experience with Toby taught me about responsibility, love, and how bravery sometimes means asking for help. Although the scare was big, so was the life lesson. Toby became not only my little furry friend but also my great teacher.

We decided that Toby would stay with us. Mom said he was part of our family now, and together, we would  ensure he had a life full of love and joy.

I will close this day with a heart full of hope. The sadness I felt this morning has turned into gratitude for having more time with Toby. I know challenges will come, but I also know that, together, we can face them.

Thank you for being here in the good times and the difficult ones. Until our next adventure.

With love, learnings, and a new promise,

Lucas.

Made in United States
Orlando, FL
25 November 2024

54335319R00059